AHITI TRAVEL GUIDE

2024

Discovering Paradise: A Journey
Through Tahiti's Enchanting Beauty
and Rich Culture

Donald M. Clark

1

Table Of Content

Chapter 1: Introduction to Tahiti................................4

Overview of Tahiti... 4

History and Culture of Tahiti............................10

Geography and Climate of Tahiti...................... 15

Chapter 2: Planning Your Trip to Tahiti.................. 22

When to Visit Tahiti.. 22

How to Get to Tahiti....................................... 29

Visa Requirements for Tahiti Travel................... 36

Tahiti Accommodation Options......................... 42

Tahiti's Transportation.....................................49

Chapter 3: Exploring the Islands of Tahiti...............56

The Main Island of Tahiti.................................56

Bora Bora...64

Moorea...71

Huahine.. 78

Taha'a and Raiatea..85

Fakarava and Rangiroa...................................91

Chapter 4: Top Attractions and Activities in Tahiti..98

Beaches and Water Activities...........................98

Hiking and Exploring Nature........................... 104

Traditional Performances and Cultural Experiences.. 111

Museums and Historical Sites.........................117

Shopping and Farmers' Markets......................126

Chapter 5: Practical Information for Travelers to Tahiti.. **135**

Currency, Language, and Communication in Tahiti....

135

Travelers to Tahiti Should Know About Health and Safety.................142

Tahitian Culture's Customs and Etiquette............149

Itinerary for 7 Days in Tahiti................................. 156

Conclusion...162

Chapter 1: Introduction to Tahiti

Overview of Tahiti

Tahiti is the largest island in French Polynesia, a French overseas territory in the South Pacific Ocean. It is well-known for its breathtaking scenery, blue lagoons, and colorful culture. Tahiti is frequently seen as a dream location for those seeking a tropical paradise experience.

Tahiti is located in the Society Islands archipelago and is divided into two sections: Tahiti Nui (the larger western section) and Tahiti Iti (the smaller eastern section). The lush green slopes, volcanic summits, black sand beaches, and gushing waterfalls distinguish the island.

Papeete, the capital city of French Polynesia, is located on the northwest coast of Tahiti Nui. It is the region's commercial and administrative hub. Papeete combines modern conveniences with traditional Polynesian charm. Visitors can explore vivid markets, enjoy local cuisine, and soak up the vibrant ambiance.

Tahiti has a tropical climate with year-round temperatures ranging from 70°F to 90°F (21°C to 32°C). The island has two distinct seasons: the wet season, which lasts from November to April, and the dry season, which lasts from May to October. Visitors can enjoy excellent weather conditions in both seasons, but the dry season is often regarded as the ideal time to come.

Tahiti's magnificent natural beauty is one of its key draws. Hiking, snorkeling, diving, and exploring the island's pristine beaches are just a few of the outdoor activities available. Visitors can go on guided hikes to find secret waterfalls and panoramic views, or they can dive into crystal-clear lagoons filled with colorful aquatic life.

Tahiti also offers a diverse cultural experience. Visitors can witness traditional dance performances, listen to enchanting music, and learn about ancient customs and traditions because Polynesian culture is deeply rooted in the daily lives of the locals. Several cultural sites, including marae (sacred temples) and museums showcasing Polynesian art, history, and craftsmanship, can be found on the island.

Tahiti's accommodation options range from luxury resorts to budget-friendly guesthouses. Many resorts offer overwater bungalows, which allow guests to stay directly above the turquoise lagoons. These bungalows often feature private decks, direct access to the water, and stunning views of the surrounding nature.

Tahiti's cuisine is a delightful fusion of French and Polynesian flavors. Fresh seafood delicacies such as poisson cru (marinated raw fish) and Tahitian vanilla-infused dishes are available to visitors. The island also produces its unique rum and offers a variety of tropical fruits like pineapple, mango, and papaya.

To reach Tahiti, most international travelers arrive at Faa'a International Airport, located near

Papeete. The airport serves as an inter-island hub for flights within French Polynesia. Several airlines fly to Tahiti regularly from major cities around the world.

History and Culture of Tahiti

Tahiti is an island located in the South Pacific Ocean, part of the French Polynesia territory. It is renowned for its stunning natural beauty, but it also has a rich history and vibrant culture that has shaped the identity of its people.

History

Tahiti's history dates back thousands of years when Polynesians first settled on the island. The exact origins of the early settlers are still debated, but it is believed that they arrived from Southeast Asia or the islands of Melanesia. These early inhabitants developed a unique culture and social structure.

In 1767, British explorer Samuel Wallis became the first European to set foot on Tahiti. This encounter marked the beginning of European influence on the island. In 1842, Tahiti became a French protectorate, and later in 1880, it was fully annexed by France. The French colonial period brought significant changes to Tahitian society, including the introduction of Christianity and Western education.

During World War II, Tahiti played a strategic role as a military base for the United States. After the war, tourism started to flourish on the island, leading to further development and modernization.

Culture

Tahitian culture is deeply rooted in its Polynesian heritage. The people of Tahiti have preserved many ancient traditions and customs throughout the centuries. One of the most iconic aspects of Tahitian culture is its music and dance.

Traditional Tahitian music often features rhythmic drumming accompanied by ukuleles and guitars. The songs tell stories of love, nature, and daily life. The most famous form of dance in Tahiti is called "Ori Tahiti" or Tahitian dance. It involves fast hip-shaking movements, graceful hand gestures, and vibrant costumes adorned with flowers.

Another essential element of Tahitian culture is its cuisine. Traditional dishes often incorporate fresh seafood such as tuna, mahi-mahi, and coconut-based ingredients. The national dish of Tahiti is called "poisson cru," which is a raw fish salad marinated in lime juice and coconut milk.

Tahitian arts and crafts are also highly valued. The people of Tahiti are skilled in woodcarving, weaving, and tattooing. Intricate designs and patterns are commonly found in their artwork, reflecting their connection to nature and ancestral spirits.

Family and community play a central role in Tahitian culture. The concept of "mana," which represents spiritual power, is deeply ingrained in the society. Respect for elders, hospitality, and communal harmony are highly valued virtues.

Geography and Climate of Tahiti

Tahiti is a captivating destination located in the South Pacific Ocean. It is the largest island in French Polynesia and serves as the economic, cultural, and political center of the archipelago. Known for its stunning landscapes, turquoise waters, and vibrant culture, Tahiti offers a unique blend of natural beauty and traditional Polynesian charm. Understanding the geography and climate of Tahiti is essential for travelers looking to explore this tropical paradise.

Geography of Tahiti

Tahiti is part of the Society Islands group, which is composed of five main islands: Tahiti, Moorea, Bora Bora, Huahine, and Raiatea. The island of Tahiti itself is divided into two parts: Tahiti Nui (the larger portion) and Tahiti Iti (the smaller portion). The capital city, Papeete, is located on the northwest coast of Tahiti Nui.

Tahiti Nui is characterized by its steep landscape, dominated by Mount Orohena, the highest point in French Polynesia. Lush valleys, cascading waterfalls, and deep ravines are dispersed throughout this region. On the other side, Tahiti Iti boasts rocky cliffs, gorgeous beaches, and isolated coves.

Climate of Tahiti

Tahiti features a tropical climate with mild temperatures year-round. The island sees two distinct seasons: a wet season from November to April and a dry season from May to October.

During the wet season, Tahiti receives a larger amount of rainfall. Showers are frequent but usually short-lived, followed by sunny skies. These rain showers contribute to the luxuriant vegetation that blankets the island during this period. Temperatures range from 77°F (25°C) to 86°F (30°C), providing a suitable setting for outdoor activities.

The dry season in Tahiti provides less rainfall and lower humidity levels. Days are often bright and pleasant, with temperatures ranging from 73°F (23°C) to 84°F (29°C). This season is considered the peak tourist season because of the great weather conditions.

Influences on Climate

Tahiti's climate is influenced by various variables, including its location in the South Pacific Ocean and the occurrence of trade winds. The island lies slightly below the equator, which means it experiences a tropical environment throughout the year.

The trade winds, sometimes known as "Alizés," blow from the southeast, bringing cool breezes and reducing temperatures. These winds also help to generate rain clouds, particularly during the wet season when they interact with moisture from the ocean.

Tahiti's climate is also influenced by its location. Because the mountains act as barriers, rainfall is dispersed unevenly across the island. The windward side, which faces east, receives more precipitation than the leeward side, resulting in a noticeable variation in vegetation and scenery.

Biodiversity and Topography

Tahiti's unique geography supports a diverse range of habitats and species. This island paradise is rich in natural treasures, from lush jungles to pristine coral reefs.

Tahiti Nui's hilly regions are covered in lush rainforests abounding with indigenous plant species. These forests are home to a variety of birds, insects, and fauna. Hiking routes allow guests to uncover secret waterfalls and stunning perspectives while exploring this green region.

Tahiti's coastal areas are distinguished by beautiful beaches and vivid coral reefs. During certain seasons, snorkeling and diving aficionados can immerse themselves in an underwater world teeming with colorful fish, sea turtles, and even dolphins or whales.

Chapter 2: Planning Your Trip to Tahiti

When to Visit Tahiti

Tahiti is a tropical paradise in French Polynesia known for its magnificent scenery, crystal-clear oceans, and colorful culture. When planning a vacation to Tahiti, it is critical to consider the optimum time to visit to make the most of your time there. Weather conditions, tourist throngs, and price can all have a significant impact on the whole experience. Based on these criteria, our thorough travel guide will offer you complete information on when to visit Tahiti.

Climate Conditions

Tahiti has a warm and tropical environment all year, making it an appealing destination for those seeking sun and leisure. It should be noted, however, that the region has two separate seasons: the dry season and the wet season.

Tahiti's dry season lasts from May to October and is typically regarded as the finest time to visit. During this time, the weather is sunny with low humidity and colder temperatures ranging from 70°F (21°C) to 80°F (27°C). The sea is also calmer at this time, making it excellent for water activities like snorkeling and diving.

The wet season in Tahiti, on the other hand, lasts from November to April. Higher temperatures, greater humidity, and intermittent rain define this time. While it may rain often during this time of year, showers are typically brief and are followed by sunny skies. Despite the rain, the wet season provides lush flora and the opportunity to see spectacular waterfalls at their best.

Crowds of Tourists

Another issue to consider while arranging a vacation to Tahiti is the number of tourists. Tahiti's peak tourism season runs from May to October when visitors from all over the world travel to experience the island's natural splendor. Popular sights may be crowded during this period, and hotel rates may be higher.

Consider visiting Tahiti during the shoulder seasons for a more intimate and calm experience. The months of April and November provide a wonderful balance of good weather and fewer visitors. While skipping the peak tourist season, you can still enjoy good temperatures and participate in a variety of activities.

Considerations for the Budget

When planning any trip, the budget is an important consideration. Tahiti is recognized as a premium location, and rates can be higher than in other parts of the region. Tahiti can, however, be visited on a budget with careful planning.

Accommodation prices tend to be lower during the low season, which runs from November to April, and you may be able to get better discounts on airfares. Moreover, certain resorts and hotels offer special rates during this time. If your travel dates are flexible, try scheduling your trip at this time to take advantage of cost discounts.

Festivals and Events

Tahiti has a rich cultural legacy and conducts several events and festivals throughout the year. If you want to immerse yourself in the local culture, planning your visit to coincide with these events will help.

Heivai Tahiti, a month-long celebration celebrated from late June to early August, is one of Tahiti's most well-known events. This lively celebration features traditional Polynesian dance performances, music, sporting events, and arts and crafts exhibitions. It provides a once-in-a-lifetime opportunity to experience Tahiti's rich cultural heritage.

How to Get to Tahiti

Tahiti, located in French Polynesia, is a popular tourist destination. It's no surprise that tourists come to this tropical paradise with its gorgeous beaches, blue waters, and colorful culture. It's critical to know how to get to Tahiti if you're planning a trip there. In this travel guide, we will look at the numerous transportation choices for getting to Tahiti.

By Air

The most popular mode of transportation to Tahiti is by flight. Faa'a International Airport (PPT), located in the capital city of Papeete, is the principal international gateway. Several airlines fly to Tahiti from major cities all around the world.

International Travel

Many major airlines fly to Faa'a International Airport regularly. Air France, Air New Zealand, Hawaiian carriers, Qantas Airways, and United Airlines are among the popular carriers that fly to Tahiti. Direct flights are available from locations such as Los Angeles, Paris, Auckland, Sydney, and Tokyo.

Transfer Flights

You may need to take a connecting trip if there are no direct flights from your area to Tahiti. Several airlines provide connections to Tahiti via other Pacific islands or major hubs such as Los

Angeles or Auckland. Honolulu (HNL), Auckland (AKL), Los Angeles (LAX), and Tokyo (NRT) are all popular connecting airports.

By Sea

While plane travel is the most convenient way to get to Tahiti, some visitors choose a more leisurely approach and arrive by water.

Cruise Lines

Tahiti is frequently included in cruise ship itineraries, allowing tourists to visit numerous locations in one trip. Papeete is a prominent port of call for several cruise companies sailing across the South Pacific. Consider scheduling a cruise that includes Tahiti if you want a slower-paced excursion with the added luxury of onboard amenities and activities.

Passenger and Cargo Ships

Some freight and passenger ships provide transportation to Tahiti for a more distinctive and exciting experience. Depending on the departure point, these journeys can last several weeks or even months. While this is a less common and more time-consuming option, it can be an interesting way to go to Tahiti for those looking for a genuinely off-the-beaten-path journey.

How to Get Around Tahiti

When you arrive in Tahiti, you will have several alternatives for navigating around the island.

Car Rentals

Renting a car is a popular way to see Tahiti at your leisure. There are several automobile rental firms at Faa'a International Airport and downtown Papeete. It is vital to remember that driving in Tahiti is done on the right side of the road, as it is in the United States.

Taxis

Taxis are plentiful in Tahiti, particularly near the airport and key tourist sites. However, it is recommended that you agree on the fee before beginning your journey or that the driver utilize a meter.

Transportation by Public

Tahiti has a public bus system called Le Truck that provides an inexpensive method to get about the island. These open-air buses go along predetermined routes and can be flagged down at authorized points. It's important to note that Le Truck has a limited schedule, so plan your route appropriately.

Scooters and Bicycles

Renting bicycles or scooters for shorter trips or exploring specific locations can be a fun and environmentally friendly alternative. Rental businesses can be found in Papeete and other tourist places.

Visa Requirements for Tahiti Travel

Many people wish to visit Tahiti, a lovely island in French Polynesia. However, before you plan your vacation, you should be aware of the visa requirements for entering the nation. In this detailed travel guide, we will go over the visa requirements for visiting Tahiti, including the different types of visas, the application process, and the necessary paperwork.

Visa Requirements for Tahiti Travel

Tahiti is part of French Polynesia, a French overseas collectivity. As a result, visa requirements for visitors to Tahiti vary depending on their nationality and length of stay. There are various types of visas available, and it's critical to know which one is appropriate for your travel plans.

Visas for Short-term Stays

These visas are valid for up to 90 days in Tahiti for tourists and business travelers. Short-term visas are normally not required for nationals of the European Union, the United States, Canada, Japan, and Australia. However, before traveling, make sure to check the current visa regulations for your nationality.

Visas for Extended Stays

If you intend to stay in Tahiti for more than 90 days, you must obtain a long-stay visa. This visa is typically granted for a maximum of one year and is renewable every year. You must submit proof of adequate funds to maintain yourself during your stay, a return or onward ticket, and a valid passport to acquire a long-stay visa.

Permits for Work and Dwelling

You must apply for a work and residency visa if you wish to work or live in Tahiti. A specific employment offer, verification of professional qualifications, and a medical certificate are required as part of the application procedure. The permit is usually valid for one year and can be renewed every year.

The Application Procedure

To apply for a visa or permission, fill out the necessary application form and send it to the nearest French Consulate or Embassy.

Depending on your country, the application process may differ, but in general, you will need to present the following documents:

- A valid passport with at least two blank pages, as well as a passport-sized photograph

- A filled-out visa application form

- Proof of lodging (such as a hotel reservation or rental agreement)

- A return or connecting ticket

- Proof of adequate finances to meet your costs throughout your stay

- A medical certificate (if applying for a job and stay permit)

Fees and Processing Time

Visa application processing times vary depending on the kind of visa and the consulate or embassy. To avoid delays, you must apply well in advance of your travel date. Visa fees differ depending on your nationality and the type of visa you seek. It is recommended that you check the current fee schedule for your nationality on the website of the French Consulate or Embassy.

Understanding the visa requirements for Tahiti is critical to ensuring a pleasant and trouble-free journey. You may enjoy the beauty and culture of this gorgeous island by carefully researching your visa choices and completing the requisite application process.

Tahiti Accommodation Options

Tahiti, French Polynesia's largest island, is a tropical paradise noted for its magnificent beaches, crystal-clear oceans, and teeming marine life. One of the most crucial factors to consider while organizing a trip to this gorgeous region is lodging. Tahiti has a variety of housing alternatives to suit all budgets and preferences, ranging from luxurious resorts to modest guesthouses. In this travel guide, we will look at some of the most popular forms of lodging in Tahiti.

Hotels and Resorts

Tahiti has a plethora of luxury resorts and hotels that appeal to guests looking for a high-end experience. Private overwater villas, infinity pools, spa facilities, fine dining restaurants, and access to private beaches are common features of these establishments. The St. Regis Bora Bora Resort, Four Seasons Resort Bora Bora, and InterContinental Bora Bora Resort & Thalasso Spa are among the well-known resorts in Tahiti.

Mid-range hotels are also available throughout the island for those looking for comfortable but less expensive accommodations. These hotels typically provide common amenities such as swimming pools, on-site eateries, and convenient access to neighboring attractions. Manava Suite Resort Tahiti, Hotel Sarah Nui, and Hotel Tahiti Nui are examples of mid-range hotels in Tahiti.

Bed and Breakfasts and Guesthouses

Guesthouses and bed and breakfasts are excellent choices for individuals looking for a more authentic experience or a more affordable option. These motels are frequently family-run businesses that offer a warm atmosphere and customized service. Guesthouses can be found all around Tahiti, including on popular beaches and in more remote locales.

Guesthouses usually provide pleasant rooms or bungalows with shared amenities like communal kitchens and outdoor spaces. Some may also serve meals or organize activities for their visitors. Travelers staying at a guesthouse may immerse themselves in the local culture and interact with friendly hosts who can provide insider information on touring the island.

Rentals for Vacations

Vacation rentals, which comprise private villas, flats, or houses accessible for short-term visits, are another popular lodging option in Tahiti. When compared to hotels or resorts, vacation rentals provide more space and privacy, making them ideal for families or groups of friends visiting together. These homes frequently have kitchens, living areas, and outdoor spaces such as gardens or terraces.

Booking a vacation rental provides guests with a home away from home experience, allowing them to cook their meals and spend leisurely nights in a comfortable atmosphere. Vacation rental websites like Airbnb and VRBO provide a wide choice of vacation rental alternatives in

Tahiti, allowing tourists to select based on their interests and budget.

Eco-Lodges

Eco-lodges are a fantastic choice for environmentally aware guests who want to minimize their environmental effects. These lodgings are intended to blend in with their natural surroundings while using environmentally friendly techniques. In Tahiti, eco-lodges frequently offer rustic yet cozy bungalows or cottages created from locally obtained materials.

These lodges place a premium on environmentally friendly efforts such as solar electricity, rainwater harvesting, and trash management systems. They also provide eco-tourism activities such as nature treks, snorkeling trips, and cultural encounters. Staying at an eco-lodge allows guests to enjoy Tahiti's natural beauty while also supporting environmentally responsible tourism.

Tahiti's Transportation

Tahiti's transportation is generally made possible by a combination of land and water-based types of transportation. Tahiti's main island, Tahiti Nui, has numerous options for moving around and enjoying its natural beauty, cultural sites, and bustling cities.

Vehicle Rental

Renting a car is a popular option for visitors who wish to explore the island at their speed. There are several car rental companies at Faa'a International Airport, Papeete (the capital city), and other significant cities. It is vital to note that driving in Tahiti is done on the right side of the road, and a valid international driver's license or a French driver's license is required.

Taxis

Tahiti has an abundance of taxis, which can be obtained at designated taxi stands or hailed on the street. They are a good choice for shorter trips or when traveling with a lot of bags. However, because taxis in Tahiti do not use meters, it is best to negotiate the fare before beginning the ride.

Buses for the Public

Tahiti has an extensive public bus network managed by the business "Le Truck," which provides an inexpensive method of transportation around the island. Most major towns and tourist locations, including popular beaches and cultural sites, are served by buses. Because schedules sometimes change, it is best to double-check the schedules ahead of time.

Ferries

Inter-island boats to other islands in French Polynesia are available for individuals who want to venture beyond Tahiti Nui. Papeete is home to the principal ferry port, which connects Moorea, Huahine, Raiatea, Bora Bora, and other adjacent islands. The ferry services run on set schedules and include both passenger and car transportation.

Flights inside the United States

Tahiti has multiple domestic airports, allowing for convenient air travel to other islands in French Polynesia. Air Tahiti is the principal local airline, with regular flights to places such as Moorea, Bora Bora, Huahine, Raiatea, and the outer islands. It is best to book domestic flights in advance, especially during peak tourist seasons.

Rental of Bicycles

Bicycle rental services are offered in several locations in Tahiti for eco-conscious guests or those who prefer a more active way of transportation. Cycling is a fun way to see the island's gorgeous coastline roads and lush surroundings. It is crucial to note, however, that the terrain in Tahiti can be mountainous in some locations, so it is best to choose routes that suit individual fitness levels.

It is worth noting that the transportation infrastructure in Tahiti may not be as comprehensive as in some developed areas. As a result, it is best to prepare ahead of time and give enough of time for transit between different areas on the island. Furthermore, traffic congestion can develop at peak hours in major cities such as Papeete.

It is critical to consider local customs and etiquette when traveling within Tahiti. In Tahitian society, politeness and respect are highly valued. When entering public buses or taxis, it is traditional to greet the driver or fellow passengers with a friendly "Ia ora na" (hello) or "Mauruuru" (thank you).

Finally, transportation in Tahiti provides a variety of options to accommodate a variety of preferences and budgets. Visitors can explore the island easily and comfortably by vehicle, taxi, bus, boat, or aircraft while experiencing the gorgeous landscapes and unique cultural experiences that Tahiti has to offer.

Chapter 3: Exploring the Islands of Tahiti

The Main Island of Tahiti

Tahiti Nui, or the Main Island of Tahiti, is the largest and most populous island in French Polynesia. It is situated in the middle Pacific Ocean, about 4,000 kilometers (2,500 miles) southeast of Hawaii. Tahiti is well-known for its beautiful scenery, colorful culture, and friendly people, making it a popular destination for those looking for a tropical paradise.

Climate and Geography

Tahiti is divided into two sections: Tahiti Nui (Big Tahiti) and Tahiti Iti (Little Tahiti). Dramatic mountain peaks, lush valleys, gushing waterfalls, and black sand beaches characterize the island. Mount Orohena is the highest point in French Polynesia, towering at 2,241 meters (7,352 ft).

Tahiti has a tropical environment, with warm temperatures all year. The temperature usually fluctuates between 24 and 30 degrees Celsius (75 and 86 degrees Fahrenheit). The rainy season lasts from November to April, with significant downpours on occasion. From May to October, the dry season provides nice weather with reduced humidity levels.

People and Culture

Polynesian traditions and rituals are strongly ingrained in Tahitian culture. Polynesians, who are famed for their warmth and hospitality, make up the majority of the local population. Although English is frequently spoken in tourist areas, the official languages are French and Tahitian.

Music and dancing are important aspects of Tahitian culture. Visitors will enjoy traditional performances that include strong drumming rhythms and elegant hip-shaking dances. The Heiva festival, held in July each year, celebrates the finest of Tahitian culture through music, dancing competitions, sporting events, and traditional artisan shows.

Activities and Attractions

Tahiti has a diverse assortment of attractions and activities to suit a variety of interests and tastes. Here are a few highlights:

Papeete

Papeete, Tahiti's main city, is a vibrant and busy hub with a combination of modern conveniences and traditional charm. Visitors can enjoy exquisite Polynesian cuisine while exploring local markets, art galleries, and museums.

Sports on the Water

Tahiti is a water sports enthusiast's heaven, with its crystal-clear lagoons and plentiful marine life. Snorkeling, scuba diving, paddleboarding, and kayaking are popular activities for exploring the vibrant underwater world.

Nature and Hiking

Tahiti's mountainous topography offers numerous options for trekking and exploring nature. The Fautaua Valley has scenic pathways that lead to the Fautaua Waterfall, while the Papenoo Valley has lush vegetation and breathtaking scenery.

Beaches with Black Sand

Tahiti is famous for its black sand beaches, which are the result of volcanic activity. Matavai Bay and Lafayette Beach are two popular places for travelers to unwind and soak up the rays.

Cultural Encounters

Visit marae (old temples), attend traditional rites, or participate in courses to learn traditional crafts such as weaving or tattooing to immerse yourself in Tahitian culture.

Transportation and Lodging

Faa'a International Airport (PPT) in Tahiti serves as a key gateway to French Polynesia. Several airlines provide direct flights from major cities worldwide.

Tahiti's accommodation options range from luxurious resorts to budget-friendly guesthouses. Most hotels are concentrated around Papeete and its vicinity, however, there are also options accessible in other sections of the island.

Tahiti's main island is a tropical paradise with a wide choice of sights and activities. Tahiti has something for everyone, from magnificent scenery and pristine beaches to vibrant culture and kind hospitality. This gorgeous island will captivate your senses and leave you with amazing memories, whether you want adventure, leisure, or cultural encounters.

Bora Bora

Bora Bora is a beautiful island in the South Pacific, specifically in Tahiti's French Polynesia region. It is famous for its spectacular natural beauty, opulent resorts, and crystal-clear turquoise waters. Bora Bora has become a popular honeymoon resort, as well as an adventurous location for people wishing to relax in a tropical paradise.

Climate and Geography

Bora Bora is located in the Society Islands archipelago, some 230 kilometers (143 miles) northwest of Papeete, the capital of French Polynesia. The island is encircled by a lagoon and a barrier reef, which creates a haven for marine life and adds to the attractive environment. Mount Otemanu, an extinct volcano, dominates the landscape of the island with its unmistakable peak.

Bora Bora's climate is tropical, with high temperatures and humidity throughout the year. The wet season lasts from November to April, whereas the dry season lasts from May to October. The average temperature ranges from 24°C (75°F) to 30°C (86°F), providing visitors with comfortable weather for most of the year.

Activities and Attractions

Bora Bora has a wide range of attractions and activities to suit a wide range of interests. The most recognizable aspect of the island is its magnificent lagoon, which is ideal for swimming, snorkeling, and diving. Visitors may explore spectacular coral gardens teaming with colorful fish, rays, sharks, and other marine life thanks to the clear waters.

Bora Bora offers a variety of water sports, including jet skiing, paddleboarding, kayaking, and sailing. For those looking for an adrenaline rush, many resorts offer exhilarating sports such as parasailing and kiteboarding.

Visitors can go on a shark and ray feeding expedition for a one-of-a-kind experience. Participants on this guided excursion can swim alongside blacktip reef sharks and stingrays in their native habitat, affording an unparalleled interaction with these spectacular species.

Exploring the verdant interior of the island is a must. Hiking trails lead to panoramic views from where visitors can gaze out over the lagoon and nearby islands. Cultural excursions can provide insights into the local way of life, such as traditional crafts, music, and dancing.

Accommodations and Meals

Bora Bora is well-known for its opulent resorts that provide world-class lodgings and facilities. The island's distinguishing feature is its overwater villas set on stilts over the lagoon. These exclusive getaways offer direct access to the crystal-clear seas as well as breathtaking views of the surrounding natural splendor.

Bora Bora resorts also provide outstanding dining options, ranging from fine international cuisine to traditional Polynesian fare. Many restaurants include fresh seafood, such as tuna, mahi-mahi, and lobster, allowing tourists to embark on a culinary excursion.

How to Get Around

Bora Bora is accessible by Faa'a International Airport in Papeete, Tahiti. Travelers can then get a domestic aircraft to Bora Bora Airport, which is located on a motu (little islet) near the main island. Alternatively, several luxury resorts provide private boat or helicopter transports directly from Tahiti.

Taxis, rental cars, bicycles, and even electric-powered boats are available once on the island. However, it's worth noting that Bora Bora is a small island that may be explored on foot or by bicycle.

Bora Bora, with its magnificent natural beauty, luxurious accommodations, and a wide selection of activities for all sorts of travelers, provides a genuinely perfect tropical holiday. Whether you want to rest on gorgeous beaches or go on exhilarating water adventures, this Tahiti paradise will provide an amazing experience.

Moorea

Moorea is a beautiful island in the South Pacific that is part of the Society Islands group in French Polynesia. It is only a short distance northwest of Tahiti, French Polynesia's largest and most populous island. Moorea is known as the "Magical Island" because of its magnificent natural beauty, attractive sceneries, crystal-clear blue waters, and lush green mountains.

Climate and Geography

Moorea is formed like a heart and covers an area of approximately 52 square miles (134 square kilometers), with two deep bays, Cook's Bay and Opunohu Bay, slicing into its northern coast. The island is bordered by a lush coral reef teeming with marine life, making it a popular snorkeling and diving destination. Moorea's scenery is defined by stunning volcanic peaks, like as Mount Tohivea, which stands 3,960 feet (1,207 meters) tall.

Moorea has a tropical climate with mild temperatures all year. The average temperature ranges from 75°F (24°C) to 85°F (29°C), making it ideal for outdoor activities. It is crucial to remember, however, that Moorea has two separate seasons: a dry season from May to October and a wet season from November to April. Showers and tropical storms are common throughout the wet season, but they are usually brief.

How to Get There

Most visitors arrive in Moorea via Faa'a International Airport on the adjoining island of Tahiti. They can then take a short domestic flight or a ferry to Moorea. The ferry ride takes around 30 minutes and provides breathtaking views of the neighboring islands and lagoons.

Accommodations

Moorea has a variety of accommodations to meet the needs and interests of any guest. There is something for everyone, from luxurious resorts and overwater bungalows to intimate guesthouses and budget-friendly hotels. Many Moorea resorts are located on the water's edge, providing direct access to the island's gorgeous beaches and turquoise lagoons. Popular hotels include the Hilton Moorea Lagoon Resort &

Spa, the InterContinental Moorea Resort & Spa, and the Sofitel Moorea Ia Ora Beach Resort.

Attractions and Activities

Moorea has a plethora of activities and attractions to offer visitors. Here are a few of the highlights:

Scuba Diving and Snorkeling

Explore Moorea's brilliant coral reefs and discover a colorful underwater world teeming with tropical fish, rays, and even sharks. The crystal-clear waters give exceptional visibility, making it a snorkeler and diver's dream.

Nature Hikes and Walks

Put on your hiking boots and explore the lush interior of the island. Various routes take you to breathtaking views, secret waterfalls, and ancient archaeological sites. Nature lovers will enjoy the Belvedere Lookout and the Three Coconut Trail.

Sports on the Water

Utilize the island's quiet lagoons by participating in water sports like as paddleboarding, kayaking, jet skiing, or sailing. For those looking for action on the water, many resorts provide equipment rentals and guided tours.

Cultural Encounters

Attend traditional dance performances, explore local markets, or take a culinary class to learn how to produce real Tahitian foods and immerse yourself in the rich Polynesian culture.

Tours of the Islands

Take a guided tour of Moorea to discover its hidden treasures. Learn about the island's agricultural businesses by visiting pineapple plantations, vanilla farms, and pearl farms. You can also go on a boat tour to see hidden beaches and swim with dolphins in their natural habitat.

Moorea, Tahiti, is a dream location that combines natural beauty, adventure, and leisure. Moorea has something for everyone, whether you're looking for an adrenaline rush or a relaxing vacation. Moorea is a dream location worth visiting, from its breathtaking landscapes and vivid coral reefs to its rich cultural legacy.

Huahine

Huahine is a beautiful island in French Polynesia, more especially the Society Islands archipelago. It is located on the island of Tahiti, roughly 110 miles northwest of the main city of Papeete. Huahine, known for its pristine beaches, lush scenery, and rich cultural legacy, is also known as the "Garden of Eden" or the "Wild Island."

Climate and Geography

Huahine is made up of two major islands: Huahine Nui (Big Huahine) and Huahine Iti (Small Huahine), which are linked by a bridge. Huahine has a total land area of about 40 square miles, making it a modest island in comparison to others in French Polynesia. The scenery includes magnificent mountains, lush valleys, and crystal-clear lakes.

Huahine has a tropical climate with mild temperatures all year. The average temperature in the winter ranges from 77°F (25°C) to 86°F (30°C) in the summer. The rainy season lasts from November to April, with short but strong rainfall being prevalent. From May to October, the dry season provides more steady weather with less rainfall and lower humidity.

History and Culture

Huahine has a diverse cultural heritage that is heavily based on Polynesian traditions. The island is famous for its well-preserved archeological ruins, ancient marae (holy shrines), and hundreds-year-old stone fish traps. Visitors can explore these historical places and learn about the intriguing history of the island.

The people of Huahine are kind and proud of their cultural history. On the island, traditional crafts such as weaving, carving, and tattooing are still practiced. Visitors can interact with locals and experience their warm welcome firsthand.

Attractions and Activities

Visitors to Huahine can enjoy a variety of activities and attractions. The natural splendor of the island provides numerous chances for outdoor activities. Divers and snorkelers can explore the beautiful coral reefs abounding with marine life. Kayaking, paddleboarding, and sailing are all popular in the lagoons that surround Huahine.

Hiking routes lead to panoramic viewpoints with amazing views of the island for those who prefer land-based activities. Huahine also has a diverse tropical flora and wildlife, making it a nature lover's delight.

Another feature of a trip to Huahine is exploring the local villages. Fare, Huahine Nui's largest settlement, has quaint stores selling local handicrafts and souvenirs. Maeva is well-known for its archaeological sites and traditional Polynesian homes.

Accommodation and Meals

Huahine offers a variety of lodging alternatives to accommodate a variety of tastes and budgets. Visitors have the option of staying in luxury resorts, boutique hotels, guesthouses, or vacation rentals. Many of these properties have beautiful lagoon views or direct beach access.

The island also has a rich food scene, with traditional Polynesian delicacies as well as cosmopolitan fare. Fresh seafood, tropical fruits, and other native delights may be found at various restaurants and food stalls throughout the island.

Transportation

Visitors can fly into Huahine-Fare Airport (HUI) from Tahiti or other adjacent islands. Air Tahiti operates regularly scheduled flights. Rental automobiles, bicycles, scooters, and guided tours are available once on the island. Because of the island's small size, it is possible to visit all of its attractions in a short amount of time.

Overall, Huahine is a French Polynesia hidden gem that offers the right blend of natural beauty, cultural legacy, and relaxation. Whether you desire action or relaxation, this tropical paradise has something for everyone.

Taha'a and Raiatea

Raiatea and Taha'a are two lovely islands in French Polynesia's Society Islands group, specifically in the Tahiti archipelago. These islands provide a one-of-a-kind and magical experience for visitors seeking a mix of natural beauty, cultural immersion, and adventure.

Raiatea, sometimes known as the "Sacred Island," is French Polynesia's second-largest island. It has a rich history and is regarded as the region's cultural and religious center. Taputapuatea marae (old Polynesian temple), which is a UNESCO World Heritage site, is one of the primary attractions of Raiatea. This historic place was formerly a center for religious rites and a stopping point for Pacific journeys.

Visitors can visit the marae and learn about its historical significance in Polynesia.

Raiatea, in addition to its ancient attractions, has wonderful natural scenery. The island is surrounded by a rich coral reef, making it a popular snorkeling and diving destination. Colorful marine life abounds in the clear turquoise seas, including tropical fish, rays, and even sharks. On the island, various diving centers cater to both novice and experienced divers.

Raiatea's verdant interior is another attraction. The island is surrounded by lush mountains and valleys that are ideal for trekking and exploration. Mount Temehani provides stunning panoramic views of the surrounding islands and lagoons. Visitors can also explore Raiatea's deep rainforests, where they can come upon exotic flora and creatures.

Taha'a, also known as the "Vanilla Island," is only a short distance from Raiatea. This little island is well-known for its vanilla plantations, which produce some of the best vanilla beans in the world. Visitors visiting these estates can learn about the growing process and even engage in vanilla-themed activities like harvesting and cooking demonstrations.

Taha'a is known for its stunning white-sand beaches and crystal-clear lagoons, in addition to its vanilla plantations. Swimming, snorkeling, and kayaking are all popular water activities on the island. Visitors can explore the beautiful coral gardens and interact with a variety of marine animals. Taha'a also has several luxury resorts and boutique hotels, offering guests a calm and isolated refuge.

Visitors can participate in traditional Polynesian rites and performances to thoroughly immerse themselves in the local culture. Raiatea and Taha'a offer traditional dance and music performances, as well as handicraft workshops where tourists can make their mementos.

In terms of transportation, Raiatea and Taha'a both have airports that receive flights from Tahiti's main airport, Faa'a. There are also regular ferry services linking the islands to other adjacent French Polynesia sites.

Raiatea and Taha'a, as a whole, offer a wonderful blend of natural beauty, cultural legacy, and adventure. Whether you want a quiet beach holiday or an immersed cultural experience, these Tahiti islands provide something for everyone.

Fakarava and Rangiroa

Rangiroa and Fakarava are two beautiful atolls in French Polynesia's Tuamotu Archipelago. These distant and unspoiled locations allow tourists to immerse themselves in the South Pacific's natural splendor. Rangiroa and Fakarava are true paradises for nature lovers and adventure seekers, with turquoise lagoons teeming with marine life and unspoiled white-sand beaches.

Rangiroa and Fakarava Overview

Rangiroa, which means "vast sky" in local Polynesian, is the largest atoll in French Polynesia and one of the world's largest. It is famous for its beautiful lagoon, which runs for

110 miles (177 kilometers) and is dotted with numerous motus (small islets). Rangiroa is a famous diving site due to its abundant marine life, which includes dolphins, sharks, manta rays, and vivid coral reefs.

In contrast, Fakarava is a UNESCO Biosphere Reserve noted for its outstanding marine biodiversity. The atoll has one of the world's largest populations of grey reef sharks and is an important breeding place for uncommon species like the humphead wrasse. Fakarava's natural beauty draws eco-tourists and nature lovers looking for a pristine environment.

How to Get There

Visitors can fly into Papeete, the capital of French Polynesia and located on the island of

Tahiti, to access Rangiroa and Fakarava. Both atolls have regular domestic flights from Papeete. The journey from Papeete to Rangiroa takes about an hour, whereas the flight from Rangiroa to Fakarava takes around an hour and 30 minutes. Alternatively, ferry services connecting the islands are available, giving a lovely and relaxing way to travel.

Accommodation

Rangiroa and Fakarava have a variety of lodging alternatives to meet a variety of budgets and interests. There is something for everyone, from magnificent overwater bungalows to quaint guesthouses. Many resorts in both atolls have direct lagoon access, letting visitors enjoy snorkeling, diving, and other water sports right outside their door.

Attractions and Activities

Snorkeling and diving

Divers will love the underwater worlds of Rangiroa and Fakarava. These atolls provide spectacular diving experiences due to their crystal-clear waters and rich marine ecosystems. The Tiputa Pass in Rangiroa is famous for its powerful currents, which attract enormous schools of sharks and other pelagic animals. Another famous dive spot is Fakarava's South Pass, where divers can experience the magnificent spectacle of hundreds of sharks gathering during feeding times.

Beaches

Rangiroa and Fakarava both have beautiful beaches with fluffy white sand and blue water. Relax on the isolated beaches, soak up the sun, and enjoy the peace of these remote paradises.

Bird Observation

Several bird species call Fakarava home, including uncommon seabirds like the red-footed booby and the great frigatebird. Bird aficionados can visit the most bird sanctuaries and witness these amazing species in their natural habitat.

Cultural Encounters

Visit surrounding communities and participate in traditional activities such as dance performances, handicraft workshops, and "Tamaaraa" feasts to immerse yourself in Polynesian culture.

When is the best time to visit?

The dry season, which lasts from May to October, is the greatest time to visit Rangiroa and Fakarava. During this time, the weather is mostly bright with little rain. The water visibility for diving and snorkeling is also excellent, allowing visitors to fully appreciate the atolls' underwater treasures.

Chapter 4: Top Attractions and Activities in Tahiti

Beaches and Water Activities

Tahiti is a South Pacific tropical paradise noted for its beautiful beaches and crystal-clear waters. Tahiti provides an exceptional experience for beach lovers and adventure seekers alike, with its magnificent landscapes, active marine life, and plenty of water activities.

Tahiti's Beaches

Tahiti has many beautiful beaches that cater to a variety of tastes. Matira Beach, on the island of Bora Bora, is one of the most popular. Matira

Beach, with its pure white sand and turquoise waves, is often regarded as one of the most beautiful beaches in the world. La Plage de Maui, located on Tahiti's west coast, is another must-see beach. This black sand beach stands out against the beautiful flora and offers great options for sunbathing and swimming.

Tahiti Water Activities

Tahiti has a variety of aquatic sports for visitors to discover its beautiful marine life. Snorkeling is a popular activity, with many locations featuring vibrant coral reefs filled with tropical fish. The lagoons surrounding Tahiti are also ideal for scuba diving, with divers able to discover underwater caverns, shipwrecks, and a variety of marine creatures.

Tahiti provides exhilarating possibilities such as jet skiing and parasailing for those wanting more adrenaline-pumping adventures. Jet skiing allows you to explore secluded coves and remote beaches while speeding across the crystal-clear waters. As you soar over the water tethered to a parachute, you get a bird's-eye view of the gorgeous coastline.

Surfers will discover nirvana at Tahiti's world-famous surf breaks. Teahupo'o, located on Tahiti's southwest coast, is noted for its big waves, which draw elite surfers from all over the world. There are also beginner-friendly areas where you can take lessons and ride gentler waves if you're new to surfing.

Tahiti's Top 5 Beaches and Water Activities:

Bora Bora's Matira Beach

Matira Beach, known for its pure white sand and crystal-clear waves, is a must-see for beachgoers. Popular activities include snorkeling and swimming in the Blue Lagoon.

The Maui Beach (Tahiti)

This black sand beach provides a one-of-a-kind and stunning backdrop for swimming and sunbathing. Because of the tranquil seas, it is great for families with children.

Tahiti Teahupo'o

Teahupo'o, one of the world's most difficult surf breakers, attracts professional surfers looking for exhilarating and enormous waves. It's awe-inspiring to see the pros ride these massive swells.

Moorea Lagoonarium (Moorea) is a lagoon on the island of Moorea

The Moorea Lagoonarium, located on the nearby island of Moorea, provides a unique opportunity to swim with numerous marine animals such as sharks, stingrays, and beautiful tropical fish. Snorkelers and animal lovers will have a wonderful experience.

Tahiti Jet Skiing

Exploring the shoreline of Tahiti on a jet ski is a thrilling experience. Jet skiing allows you to see the island's splendor from a different angle, from isolated beaches to secret coves.

Hiking and Exploring Nature

Tahiti, recognized for its spectacular natural beauty and lush landscapes, has a plethora of hiking and outdoor exploring options. This tropical paradise is a dream location for outdoor enthusiasts, with breathtaking mountains and gorgeous waterfalls. Tahiti has something for everyone, whether you are an experienced hiker or simply want to immerse yourself in the beauties of nature.

Tahiti Hiking Trails

Tahiti has a wide range of hiking routes to suit all skill levels and interests. The Fautaua Valley Trail, located just outside of Papeete, the capital city, is one of the most popular. This walk winds through lush rainforests, and past flowing waterfalls, and provides beautiful views of the surrounding mountains and valleys.

The Aorai Mountain Trail is an excellent alternative for those looking for a more difficult hike. This trail leads to the peak of Mount Aorai, which stands at 2,066 meters (6,778 ft). You'll see a variety of flora and fauna along the trip, including endemic species found only in Tahiti.

The Papenoo Valley is another popular trekking location. This large valley has several routes that allow you to explore its difficult landscape and discover hidden jewels like ancient archaeological sites and delightful bathing holes. Papenoo Valley's routes range from moderate walks to arduous treks, making it appropriate for hikers of all abilities.

Tahiti Nature Explorations

Tahiti, in addition to hiking paths, has several chances for environmental expeditions that allow tourists to immerse themselves in the island's natural treasures. The Fautaua Waterfall, located in the Fautaua Valley, is one such experience. This majestic waterfall rushes down more than 300 meters (984 feet) into a pool below, providing a breathtaking picture. Visitors can enjoy the stunning surroundings while learning about the local flora and animals on guided tours to the waterfall.

Te Faaiti National Park is another must-see site for environment lovers. This park encompasses a large amount of natural rainforest, which is home to a diverse range of plant and animal species. Guided tours are available, allowing visitors to learn about Tahiti's unique ecosystem and conservation initiatives.

Tahiti has excellent snorkeling and diving options for people interested in marine life. The island is surrounded by brilliant coral reefs that are home to a plethora of colorful fish, sea turtles, and other marine species. Exploring these underwater ecosystems is an excellent way to enjoy Tahiti's natural beauty from a new angle.

Hiking and Nature Exploration Tips in Tahiti:

- Always check the weather forecast before setting out on a hike, and be prepared for sudden weather changes.

- Wear suitable hiking equipment, such as sturdy shoes, a hat, and sunscreen.

- Bring extra water and snacks to keep you hydrated and energized on your hike.

- Respect the environment by adhering to authorized pathways and avoiding disturbing wildlife or vegetation.

- Think about hiring a local guide who can provide useful information about the area's ecology, animals, and cultural value.

Tahiti has a plethora of hiking and environment exploration options. This tropical paradise delivers amazing experiences immersed in nature's beauties, whether you prefer to embark on a difficult climb or simply soak in the breathtaking view.

Traditional Performances and Cultural Experiences

Tahiti, the largest island in French Polynesia, is famous for its breathtaking natural beauty, but it also has a rich cultural past that visitors may discover through traditional performances and cultural activities. Immerse yourself in Tahitian culture's lively traditions and watch mesmerizing performances that highlight the island's history, music, dance, and art.

Performances of traditional Dance and Music

Witnessing traditional dance and music performances is one of Tahiti's most famous cultural experiences. The captivating "Ori Tahiti" dance form is an important aspect of

Tahitian culture. Dancers in bright costumes perform elaborate moves to the beats of drums and other traditional instruments. These performances frequently reflect ancient folklore, myths, and stories that have been passed down through the generations. The dancers' energetic and elegant moves are a sight to behold, captivating spectators with their skill and enthusiasm.

The Heiva Festival

The annual Heiva Festival, held in July, is a celebration of Polynesian culture. This month-long celebration features a variety of traditional acts such as dance competitions, music concerts, sporting events, and arts and crafts exhibitions. It is a fantastic opportunity to experience true Tahitian culture at its best.

Visitors can enjoy the lively environment, sample local specialties, and marvel at the skill of traditional artisans.

Maori Visits

Maraes are sacred spots that are extremely important in Tahitian culture. These old stone constructions were utilized for religious rites and social gatherings in the past. Today, certain maraes have been repaired and protected, allowing tourists to gain insight into the Tahitian people's spiritual beliefs and rituals. Guided tours provide essential information about the sites' history and cultural significance.

Workshops for Artists

Consider taking part in artisan programs where you can learn traditional crafts like weaving, carving, or painting to learn more about Tahitian culture. Skilled artists share their skills and techniques with you, allowing you to create your one-of-a-kind piece of Tahitian art. These classes offer a hands-on experience that creates a greater understanding of the island's craftsmanship and cultural legacy.

Cultural Institutions

Several cultural centers in Tahiti provide immersive experiences in traditional Tahitian culture. Through exhibitions, interactive displays, and educational activities, these facilities present a thorough overview of the island's history, customs, and traditions. Visitors can learn about tattoo meanings, ancient

Polynesian navigation techniques, and the art of tapa fabric production. Cultural institutions frequently hold live performances and workshops, allowing visitors to interact with local artists and performers.

Tahiti's cultural events and traditional performances provide a unique glimpse into French Polynesia's rich heritage. There are countless possibilities to immerse oneself in the rich traditions of the island, ranging from dance and music performances to marae visits, artisan workshops, and cultural centers. Witnessing these enthralling performances and taking part in cultural activities will leave you with a profound appreciation for the beauty and richness of Tahitian culture.

Museums and Historical Sites

Tahiti, the largest island in French Polynesia, is well-known not only for its breathtaking natural beauty but also for its rich history and cultural legacy. A variety of historical buildings and museums on the island provide tourists with an insight into Tahiti's interesting past. From ancient temples to colonial-era structures, history buffs will find much to explore in this tropical paradise.

Historic Places

Arahurahu Marae

Marae Arahurahu, located in the Paea district, is one of Tahiti's most notable archeological sites.

In traditional Polynesian civilization, this old marae (holy spot) was a hub for religious and social meetings. Visitors can observe the ruins of stone platforms, altars, and statues while learning about Tahitian rites and beliefs.

Venus's pointing

Point Venus, located on Tahiti's northern coast, is historically significant. In 1769, Captain James Cook observed the transit of Venus across the Sun, which assisted scientists in calculating the distance between the Earth and the Sun. Visitors can now examine a lighthouse built by Cook's crew and gaze out over Matavai Bay.

Home of James Norman Hall

The James Norman Hall Home in Arue is a must-see for book lovers. American novelist James Norman Hall, who co-wrote the famous novel "Mutiny on the Bounty," made Tahiti his home. The home has been preserved as a museum displaying his life and works, as well as authentic manuscripts and personal things.

Town Hall in Papeete

Tahiti's capital city, Papeete, is home to various historical landmarks, including the Town Hall. Built during French colonial control in 1890, this magnificent structure combines European and Polynesian architectural influences. Visitors can appreciate its lovely exterior and visit the interior, which has a small museum with displays of Tahitian history and culture.

Bougainville Memorial

The Bougainville Monument, located in Taravao, commemorates the arrival of Louis Antoine de Bougainville, a French explorer who discovered Tahiti in 1768. The monument includes a statue of Bougainville as well as plaques that detail his explorations and relationships with the Tahitian people.

Museums

Tahiti and Her Islands Museum

The Museum of Tahiti and Her Islands, located in Punaauia, is French Polynesia's largest museum. It provides an in-depth look at Tahitian history, culture, and natural heritage. Exhibits in the museum include prehistoric items, traditional crafts, navigational tools, and marine life displays. Visitors can also learn about how European interaction influenced Tahitian society.

Museum of Paul Gauguin

This museum in Papeari is dedicated to the great French artist Paul Gauguin. Gauguin spent several years in Tahiti, where he created some of his most famous works inspired by the landscapes and people of the island. The museum displays his paintings, sketches, and personal things, providing insight into his artistic path.

The Pearl Museum of Robert Wan

For generations, pearls have played an important role in Tahitian society. The Robert Wan Pearl

Museum, located in Papeete, shows the history and workmanship behind these priceless gems. Visitors can learn about pearl farming techniques, examine gorgeous pearl jewelry, and learn about the cultural significance of pearls in Tahitian society.

Black Pearl Museum

The Museum of Black Pearls in Papeete is another pearl museum. This one-of-a-kind museum concentrates on the growth and manufacture of black pearls, which are highly sought after due to their scarcity and beauty. Visitors can learn about pearl farming, witness live oysters, and browse a variety of pearl jewelry.

Museum of James Norman Hall

James Norman Hall is also remembered with a museum at Arue, in addition to his residence. This museum honors the author's life and accomplishments, particularly his time as a World War I pilot. Personal artifacts, photographs, and mementos from Hall's literary career and military service are on display.

Tahiti's historical landmarks and museums take tourists on a fascinating journey through time, allowing them to learn about the island's rich cultural legacy. These attractions provide a greater insight into Tahiti's past, whether by touring old marae, learning about famous explorers, or immersing oneself in the world of art and pearls.

Shopping and Farmers' Markets

Tahiti, French Polynesia's largest island, is famed not only for its magnificent natural beauty and colorful culture but also for its one-of-a-kind shopping experiences and local markets. Tahiti has a vast selection of possibilities to suit every shopper's wishes, whether they are traditional handicrafts, magnificent pearls, or exotic fruits. A thorough reference to shopping and local markets in Tahiti, from busy markets to upscale stores.

Tahiti Shopping

Tahiti has a varied selection of shopping choices for both locals and tourists. Papeete, the island's capital city, is the main shopping destination, with a wide range of stores, boutiques, and marketplaces. Smaller towns and villages dot the island and each has their own distinct shopping experiences.

Tahiti's Local Markets

Exploring Tahiti's local markets is a must-do experience for each visitor. These markets offer an authentic view of the local way of life as well as a variety of items and produce. Here are some of Tahiti's best local markets to visit:

Marché de Papeete (Papeete Market)

The Papeete Market, located in the middle of Papeete, is the largest market on the island. This bustling market, open daily, is a treasure trove of fresh fruits, vegetables, fish, spices, handicrafts, and souvenirs. It's a terrific place to learn about Tahitian culture and meet friendly locals.

Punaauia Municipal Market

This market, located just outside of Papeete in the village of Punaauia, has a more peaceful and less busy environment than the Papeete Market. Local products, flowers, arts and crafts, as well as typical Polynesian food vendors, can be found here.

Moorea Market (Marché de Moorea) is a market in Moorea, Hawaii

If you're visiting the nearby island of Moorea, don't pass up the chance to attend its local market. This market, located in the main town of Pao Pao, features a broad variety of local products, including fresh fruits & vegetables, fish, and handcrafted items. It's a terrific spot to stock up on picnic materials or locate unique gifts.

Marché de Huahine (Huahine Market)

Huahine, another beautiful French Polynesian island, has a delightful market. The Huahine Market is a tiny but vibrant market where you can buy locally grown fruits and vegetables, vanilla beans, and handcrafted items manufactured by skilled artists.

Raiatea Market (Marché de Raiatea) is a market in Raiatea, New Zealand

This lively market on the island of Raiatea provides a real shopping experience. You can shop for fresh fruit, tropical flowers, apparel, and handicrafts at the market. Local food vendors serve great traditional foods at the market.

Tahiti Shopping Experiences

Tahiti, in addition to its local markets, provides a variety of shopping experiences to suit a variety of tastes and preferences. Here are some notable Tahiti shopping destinations:

Vaima Shopping Mall

The Vaima Shopping Center, located in Papeete, is a modern structure that comprises a variety of businesses and boutiques. International brands coexist with local designers and artisans here. The complex also has restaurants and cafes, making it a handy place to stop for a breather while shopping.

The Black Pearl Market

Tahiti is famous for its stunning black pearls, and Le Marché de la Perle Noire is the ideal spot to purchase these valuable stones. This specialist market in Papeete sells a large range of black pearl jewelry, including necklaces, earrings, and bracelets. It's a great place to go if you want to bring home a one-of-a-kind and valuable souvenir.

Centers for the Arts

Tahiti is home to several artisanal centers that highlight traditional crafts and artwork. These sites allow visitors to meet local craftspeople and observe their creative processes. These centers allow purchasing real Tahitian handicrafts directly from the artists, ranging from woodcarvings and tapa cloth to paintings and sculptures.

Duty-Free Shopping

Tahiti's duty-free shops are worth browsing if you're looking for luxury goods or international names at low prices. These shops, located at the international airport and in important tourist destinations, sell a variety of things such as cosmetics, fashion, electronics, and more. Keep in mind that to benefit from duty-free prices, you must produce your passport and travel information.

Roadside Markets

You'll come across various roadside kiosks selling fresh fruits, veggies, flowers, and homemade jams as you travel about Tahiti. These stands provide a one-of-a-kind shopping experience as well as an opportunity to support local farmers and producers.

Shopping in Tahiti is an experience that mixes cultural immersion with unique treasures, whether you prefer to explore the lively markets or indulge in posh stores. Tahiti has something for any shopper's taste and budget, from traditional handicrafts to magnificent pearls.

Chapter 5: Practical Information for Travelers to Tahiti

Currency, Language, and Communication in Tahiti

Tahiti is a beautiful island in French Polynesia noted for its gorgeous landscapes, rich culture, and kind people. If you are considering a vacation to Tahiti, you must become acquainted with the local currency, language, and communication alternatives to have a pleasant and memorable time.

Currency

Tahiti's official currency is the French Pacific Franc (CFP Franc), which is denoted by the currency code XPF. The Institut d'émission d'Outre-Mer (IEOM) issues the CFP Franc, which is used not only in Tahiti but also in other French overseas territories such as New Caledonia Wallis and Futuna. Banknotes come in denominations of 500, 1,000, 5,000, and 10,000 francs, while coins come in 1, 2, 5, 10, 20, 50, and 100 francs.

While some places accept major foreign currencies such as US dollars or Euros, it is suggested to keep some CFP Francs on hand for smaller transactions or when visiting local markets.

Language

Because Tahiti is a French overseas territory, French is the official language. However, Tahitian (Reo Tahiti) is extensively spoken by the locals. Tahitian is a Polynesian language that is closely connected to other Pacific languages.

Many tourist areas, hotels, and restaurants also speak and understand English. In general, visitors will find that they can communicate well in English. Learning a few basic phrases in French or Tahitian, on the other hand, can tremendously improve your contact with the locals and demonstrate respect for their culture.

Communication

When it comes to communication choices in Tahiti, there are various solutions available to keep in touch with family and friends while on vacation. Here are some important factors to consider:

Cellular Networks

Visitors to Tahiti can use their smartphones for calls, texts, and data because the mobile network is reliable. Vodafone and VINI are the two primary mobile network operators in Tahiti. Check with your home service provider about foreign roaming prices, or try obtaining a local SIM card for lower rates.

Internet Connection

Most Tahiti hotels, resorts, and cafes provide Wi-Fi, allowing visitors to stay connected online. However, internet access may be limited or slow in more distant places or on smaller islands.

The Postal Service

You can use the local postal services to send mail or postcards from Tahiti. The major post office is in Papeete, Tahiti's capital city, and there are other smaller post offices scattered throughout the island.

Telephones in Public

While public telephones are becoming less widespread as cell phones become more prevalent, they may still be found in some locations of Tahiti. These phones frequently require a prepaid phone card, which is available at convenience stores or newsstands.

Services for Emergencies

In Tahiti, dial 15 for medical aid and 17 for police services in an emergency.

Finally, before visiting Tahiti, it is critical to have a basic awareness of the local currency, language, and communication alternatives. Familiarizing yourself with these characteristics will assist ensure a pleasant and joyful visit to this tropical paradise.

Travelers to Tahiti Should Know About Health and Safety

Tahiti is a gorgeous destination that provides visitors with a paradise-like experience. However, when visiting this lovely island, it is critical to prioritize your health and safety. You may ensure a safe and pleasurable journey to Tahiti by following a few simple guidelines.

Vaccinations and Health Screenings

It is recommended that you check with a healthcare expert or visit a travel health clinic before traveling to Tahiti to get the appropriate vaccinations. Routine immunizations, such as measles, mumps, rubella (MMR), diphtheria-tetanus-pertussis, varicella (chickenpox), and polio, should be current. Vaccinations for infections such as hepatitis A and B, typhoid, and influenza are also recommended. It is also necessary to have a basic health check-up before your vacation to ensure that you are fit to travel.

Water that is Safe to Drink

While Tahiti's tap water is typically safe to drink, it is advised to drink bottled water or employ water purification procedures such as boiling or using water purification tablets. This precaution helps to avoid stomach problems caused by unfamiliar water sources.

Protection from the Sun

Because of Tahiti's tropical climate, the sun may be fairly fierce. Even on cloudy days, it is critical to wear sunscreen with a high SPF value (30 or above) to protect yourself from damaging UV radiation. Wearing a hat, sunglasses, and lightweight clothing that covers your skin can also help to protect you from the sun's rays.

Mosquito Bite Avoidance

Tahiti is home to mosquitos that can spread diseases such as dengue fever and the Zika virus. Use insect repellents containing DEET or other authorized chemicals on exposed skin to reduce the risk of mosquito bites. Wearing long-sleeved shirts and long pants between the hours of dawn and twilight, when mosquitoes are most active, can also help. Staying in accommodations with air conditioning or screens on windows and doors can also help keep mosquitos at bay.

Ocean Security

The crystal-clear waters of Tahiti are a significant draw for visitors, but it is crucial to practice caution while swimming. Before you go swimming, learn about the local conditions and any potential hazards, such as strong currents or coral reefs. Swimming should be done only in specified areas and by any safety guidelines given by lifeguards. If you intend to participate in aquatic sports such as snorkeling or diving, be sure you have sufficient training and utilize reliable operators.

Insurance for Travel

Before visiting Tahiti, it is strongly advised that you acquire comprehensive travel insurance. Medical bills, vacation cancellations or interruptions, missing luggage, and emergency evacuation should all be covered by this insurance. Make sure to carefully study the policy specifics to understand what is and is not covered.

Local customs must be followed

Respecting Tahiti's native customs and traditions is crucial not only for cultural sensitivity but also for your safety. Learn about local customs, dress modestly when visiting religious locations, and be aware of appropriate behavior in public places.

COVID-19 Safety Precautions

COVID-19 measures are essential for travel anywhere in the world at the time of writing. Keep up to current on travel advisories and requirements issued by your home country as well as Tahiti. Follow health officials' recommendations for mask use, social distancing, and cleanliness measures.

You may have a delightful and worry-free trip to Tahiti if you follow these health and safety precautions.

Tahitian Culture's Customs and Etiquette

Tahitian culture is firmly ingrained in customs and traditions passed down through generations. Understanding and respecting local customs and etiquette is vital when visiting Tahiti since it promotes positive relationships with the locals and demonstrates admiration for their way of life. Here are some important features of Tahitian culture to remember:

Politeness and Greetings

Greetings are an integral aspect of daily interactions in Tahitian society. When meeting someone for the first time, it is usual to kiss both cheeks, beginning with the left. This is referred to as the 'haere mai' greeting. Handshakes are very popular, especially in more formal settings. When addressing elders or others of higher social position, honorific titles such as 'Monsieur' or 'Madame' are considered respectful.

The Dress Code

Tahitians dress modestly, particularly while visiting public places or attending cultural activities. Swimwear and shorts, for example, should be saved for the beach or other appropriate recreational areas. When attending traditional events or festivals, it is appropriate for women to wear long skirts or pants and for males to wear long trousers.

Tapu (Holiness)

Tapu is a Tahitian cultural concept that refers to items that are deemed sacred or taboo. Visitors should be cautious of tapu-infested areas or objects, which should not be touched or approached without permission. Visitors, for example, are not permitted to enter sacred marae (old temples) unless accompanied by a guide or given formal permission from the local community.

Giving Gifts

Gift-giving is a significant part of Tahitian culture, and it is frequently done for special events or as a token of thanks. It is customary to deliver a gift with both hands as a symbol of respect. Handmade products, local produce, and flowers are popular traditional gifts. It is vital to remember that gifts should not be opened right away.

Nature should be Respected

Tahitians have a strong connection to their natural surroundings and have a high regard for the environment. Visitors should also show their appreciation by being mindful of their influence on the land and sea. It is critical to avoid littering, destroying coral reefs, and upsetting wildlife. When participating in aquatic sports such as snorkeling or diving, it is best to adhere to local regulations and avoid touching or stepping on coral formations.

Eating Etiquette

It is usual to offer a little gift for the host, such as flowers or a bottle of wine when invited to a Tahitian home for a meal. It is polite to taste a little bit of everything that is offered and to express gratitude for the cuisine during the dinner. It is also traditional to wait for the host to finish his or her meal before beginning your own.

Language

While French is Tahiti's official language, Tahitian (Reo Tahiti) is widely spoken and has significant cultural value. Learning a few basic Tahitian phrases, such as greetings and thank expressions, can go a long way toward demonstrating respect for the local culture.

Traditional Music and Dance

Tahitian dance and music are important components of the culture and are frequently performed at significant occasions and festivities. Visitors are advised to appreciate these performances and respect them by not chatting or using technological devices during them. Applause is appropriate after each performance and expresses gratitude for the artists' talent and work.

Visitors can immerse themselves more fully in Tahitian culture and form significant ties with the islanders by adhering to certain customs and etiquette standards. Approach conversations with an open mind and a readiness to learn and adapt to the local way of life.

Itinerary for 7 Days in Tahiti

Tahiti, an exotic South Pacific island, is a haven for travelers looking for relaxation, adventure, and a taste of Polynesian culture. Tahiti, with its crystal-clear lagoons, lush green highlands, and active indigenous culture, provides a diverse selection of activities and experiences that will leave you with lasting memories. We'll take you through the best of Tahiti, from its magnificent beaches to its rich history and culture, on this 7-day trip.

Day 1: Arrival in Tahiti and Welcome

When you arrive at Faa'a International Airport, you will be met by Tahiti's warm and welcoming atmosphere. After checking into your hotel, spend some time exploring Papeete, the colorful capital city. The Municipal Market in Papeete is a lively market where you can purchase everything from fresh vegetables and seafood to local handicrafts and souvenirs. Enjoy a traditional Polynesian dance presentation and wonderful Tahitian cuisine in the evening.

Day 2: Explore Papeete and its Surrounding Area

Visit the Robert Wan Pearl Museum after breakfast to learn about the history and art of pearl farming in Tahiti. Then, proceed to the Papeete Waterfront for a stroll along the beach, taking in the magnificent views of the ocean and neighboring mountains. In the afternoon, take a short trip to the Gauguin Museum to learn about the life and works of the great Tahitian post-impressionist artist Paul Gauguin.

Day 3: Moorea's Natural Beauty

Take a ferry from Papeete to Moorea, a beautiful island noted for its beautiful beaches, lush valleys, and amazing views. Spend the day discovering Moorea's natural beauties, including the Belvedere Lookout for panoramic views of the island, the Moorea Dolphin Center for a memorable experience with these wonderful creatures, and the Opunohu Valley for a taste of the island's lush, tropical scenery.

Day 4: Moorea Adventure

On day four, take a 4x4 safari tour of Moorea, exploring the island's interior and viewing landmarks such as the Pihaa Pass, the Magic Mountain, and the Faarumai Waterfall. Rent a kayak or paddleboard in the afternoon and explore the crystal-clear waters of Moorea's lagoon, keeping an eye out for tropical fish and other marine life.

Day 5: Culture and Relaxation

Spend a quiet day at your hotel's beach or pool after a few days of action. In the afternoon, go to the Tahiti Pearl Farm to learn about the process of cultivating black pearls and possibly buy a one-of-a-kind keepsake. Enjoy a classic Polynesian luau in the evening, complete with live music, dancing, and a delectable feast.

Day 6: Bora Bora Island

Take a trip from Papeete to Bora Bora, a well-known tropical destination known for its overwater villas and turquoise lagoon. Spend the day exploring the island, stopping by the Bora Bora Museum, Mount Pahia, and the infamous Bloody Mary's Bar. Enjoy a sunset dinner cruise around the island in the evening, taking in the stunning sights and relishing the native cuisine.

Day 7: The Last Day in Paradise

Spend the morning of your final day in Tahiti lounging on the gorgeous beaches of Bora Bora, soaking up the sun and enjoying the crystal-clear waters. In the afternoon, embark on a lagoon trip where you may snorkel among the colorful corals and see a variety of aquatic life. As your Tahiti vacation comes to a close, reflect on the unique memories you've created and begin planning your next trip to this enchanting corner of the world.

Conclusion

We hope that as you reach the last pages of our Tahiti Travel Guide, the words herein have sparked a spark of wanderlust, a want to experience the remarkable. Tahiti, with its sun-kissed beaches and lively culture, is more than just a vacation spot; it's a poetry trip waiting to be written.

Tahiti, located in the heart of the South Pacific, welcomes you with open arms to explore its hidden coves, revel in its gastronomic delights, and immerse yourself in the rhythm of island life. Beyond the useful advice and insightful recommendations, this guide provides a portal to timeless moments - where the turquoise waters meet the azure sky and the warm embrace of the people becomes a treasured memory.

Remember that your journey to Tahiti is more than just a vacation; it's an odyssey of self-discovery and cultural immersion. Allow the gentle breezes of the Pacific to whisper tales of a found paradise, and may the colorful spirit of Tahiti linger with you long after you return.

Tahiti awaits your discovery, from the pristine beaches to the lush interiors, from traditional dances to new beats. As you bid farewell to these pages, revel in the prospect of the adventures that await you. The adventure may come to an end here, but the sounds of Tahiti will live on in your heart forever.

Good luck, and may your Tahitian dreams become treasured memories. May your travels be blessed with joy, wonder, and the timeless charm of Tahiti till we meet again under the tropical sun.

Made in the USA
Las Vegas, NV
10 February 2024

85579416R00085